ADOPT-A-QUOTE

A Collection of Feelings-
400 Inspirational Quotes Slogans, Poems
By & For Those Touched by Adoption

Access Press

c. 2019 by Lori Carangelo
Published by Access Press, Palm Desert, California
Previous edition:
ADOPT-A-QUOTE – Bridging the Adoption Experience
ISBN: 0-942605-04-7, 1999 softcover; 2012 e-book

DEDICATION

*This book is dedicated to
all who have been touched by adoption --
those whose voices were silenced,
and those, past and present,
who helped to make their voices heard,*

.

Printed in the United States of America
ISBN 978-0-942605-60-0

contents

2.
BIRTH MOTHERS - 55

3.
BIRTH FATHERS - 73

4.
BIRTH SIBLINGS - 85

5.
ADOPTIVE MOTHERS - 99

6.
ADOPTIVE FATHERS - 107

8.

ADOPTION AUTHORS -

INTRODUCTION

"Adopt-A-Quote" is a collection of *feelings* via 400 inspirational quotes, slogans and poems shared by adoptees, birth mothers and fathers, birth siblings, adoptive mothers and fathers, and supported by civil rights activists, philosophers, psychologists, journalists, Supreme Court Justices, scholars and others who *understand* our issues. Adopt-A-Quote is intended to provide a bridge to *understanding by sharing...* because adoption has a language all it's own.

Since 1950, the "language of adoption," has most often been silently expressed in the grief of loss, the fantasy of origins, and in passive and active searches for information and acceptance by separated family members. The adoption industry has controlled the public's perception about adoption via politically "preferred adoption language guides" published for media. As adoptees and birth parents began to connect and share their individual adoption experiences and their *feelings*, and as adoptive parents began to *hear* adoptees and birth parents, the language preferred by each of these groups began to emerge.

For instance, the term "birth mother" was coined by Lee Campbell, a mother who founded Concerned United Birthparents (CUB) in 1976. "Birthmother" was also used by psychologist Betty Jean Lifton, in her book, *"Lost and Found,"* published in 1979. In 2006, a *"The Daily Bastardette,"* an online newsletter by the adoptee activist group, Bastard Nation (BN), included a blog titled *"BJ Lifton Booted From Adoption Conference - Offensive Language Cited."* Lifton, an adoptee, and longtime activist supportive of adoptee rights, was "un-invited" from speaking at an adoption conference, simply because others felt her use of the term "birthmother" was "politically offensive." After BN's blog was published, Lifton was re-invited but understandably declined. Lifton later stated that she had since lived to regret "stigmatizing" mothers with the term that some likened to a "breeder" supplying babies to meet the market's demand.

Similarly, over time, "birth" mother/father, "birth" parents and "adoptive parents" have been re-placed by various groups in favor of "natural" mother/father, "first" mother, "biological" family, "adopters," "custodial parents," "extended" family, or, simply, "mother, father, parents." Use of terms in this book are as originally used by the authors quoted or for clarity and no less respectful.

I have taken the liberty of adding captions to quotes that had none, and effort has been made to try to determine and include the adoptive status of those quoted. But in some instances, familiar quotes continue to be credited only to "Anonymous" or "Unknown."

Yours in search and discovery,
-- THE AUTHOR

1:
ADOPTEES

ADOPTION MYTH #1:
"They won't know the difference."
[Excuse for not telling a child s/he is adopted,
enabled by falsified birth certificate; even some "late
discovery"adoptees had sensed feeling out of place]

ADOPTION, A CLOSED BOOK

"Goodbyes hurt when the story is not finished
and the book has been closed forever."
--dgreetings.com

RE-WRITING HIS-STORY

"Adoption creates a split
between a person's biology and biography."
--LavenderLuz.com
("This Is Us And How To Heal It")

MISSING CHAPTER

"Being adopted is like having blank pages
in the first chapter of your life."
--Facebook *("How It Feels To Be Adopted")*

A LIFE SENTENCE

"Adoption isn't just a childhood experience,
it's a lifelong experience."
--DaShanne Stokes

HERITABILITY

"All the work on heritability
was never based on looking at genes;
it was based on the similarity
between identical twins
or between parents and children.
Now that geneticists can look at genes,
they can't find that genes account for
more than 10% of the *variation* in any human trait."
--Jerome Kagan

ADOPTEE TO ADOPTEE

"When many adoptees see others
who have been separated
from their families of origin,
our hearts hurt,
and oftentimes it's helpful
to verbally express that pain.
Regardless of the scenario,
we are saying one thing: This hurts –
Yet for just a moment,
we don't feel as alone."
--Ferera Swan

FEELINGS

"I could never share my feelings growing up
yet they wonder why I'm angry."
-Adult Adoptee, Facebook post
(*"How It Feels To Be Adopted)*

NEVER TOO OLD

"I am 60 years old
and still grieving for my birth mother."
--Catherine Sale, Adoptee
("Musings of the Lame," 1-9-17)

UNDERSTANDING ADOPTEES

"There is a story behind every person.
There is always a reason
why they are the way they are.
Think about that,
and respect them for what they are."
--MarcAndAngel

IMAGINE

"Most people couldn't imagine
losing their mother, father, brothers sisters.
aunts, uncles and grandparents
on the same day –
Yet you expect us to glorify this experience
and even celebrate it with 'gotcha days."
--*("Dear Adoption")*

PRETENDING

"I lost my family.
Everyone around me pretends they don't exist."
-Facebook post (*"Adoption Trauma"*)

I EXIST

"People are not secrets."
--Mimeo.com

MORE THAN ONE MOTHER AND FATHER

"We know that a mother and father
can love more than one child.
So why is it so hard to understand that a child
can love more than one mother and father?"
--(*"America Adopts"*)

HE SAID, SHE SAID

"He said: 'You just see me as
your son who was stolen for adoption.'
She said: 'Well, it's why you see *her* as 'Mom'
and me *not* as who I am."
--Lori Carangelo, birth mother

"She said: 'You know you focus too much
on adoption…'
She replied: 'Well, I am adopted. It is who I am.'"
--Jennifer, adoptee (*"Who Am I Really?"*)

TWO LIVES

"I'm torn between 2 lives:
the past, and what could have been
vs.
the present, and what is."
-beingadopted

WHAT GOES AROUND COMES AROUND

"It was a Catholic priest who told my adopter
that I had 'bad blood' because my mom
was a prostitute.
I got that shoved down my throat for years
because of this priest.
When I became an adult, he damned me to hell
in front of other people
for getting a divorce –
and then he died,
naked, in his housekeeper's bed."
--Gen Goad, adoptee, 10-4-00

COUNTERFEIT

"A Counterfeit—A Plated Person
I would not be-
Whatever the strata of Iniquity
My nature underlie--
Truth is good Health--and Safety, and the Sky--
How meager, what an Exile--is a Lie-
And Vocal--when we die."
--Emily Dickinson

I WONDER

"I wonder if she held me
In her warm embrace.
I wonder if I ever saw
A smile upon her face.
I wonder if they took me
From her loving arms.
I wonder if I look like her
And have her many charms."
--Gen Camper, adoptee and mother

I WONDER, TOO

"Does she know my soul is empty,
That she's missing from my heart?
Oh how I'd love to find her
So the healing can start.
I wonder if she has cried for me
As I have cried for her.
Does she ever wonder
about her little girl."
--Gen Goad, adoptee and mother

ADOPTEES' QUESTIONS

"Adoptees always have these questions.
When you're all grown up,
can't you know who you are?"
--Coco Brush, birth mother
founder, "*ANSWERS*"

BIRTHDAYS

"I wonder how my birth parents feel
when my birthday comes around."
--Tumblr (*"Confessions of an Adoptee"*)

THE NON-EVENT

"I was not allowed to talk about being adopted
when I was growing up.
I walked around feeling like I was going to explode."
--Michael Ncqvist (*"Lifeback Quotes"*)

IF THEY LOVE ME

"I would rather know
my hard core history (my truth)
than be lied to, my entire life,
by those who are supposed to
love me the most."
-Facebook (*"How It Feels To Be Adopted"*)

EXPECTATION OF GRATITUDE

"Adoption loss is the only trauma in the world
where the victims are expected
by the whole of society
to be grateful."
--Reverend Keith C. Griffith, MBE

ETERNALLY GRATEFUL

"We have no rights or say in anything.
So why should we be expected to be eternally grateful
to those involved?"
--Rebekah Hutson, adoptee

ADOPTION MYTH #2:
"The chosen child."

"I was *'chosen'* not 'born'…
because of how adopters present this,
I am one of many adoptees who pictured themselves
At a supermarket with their adopters browsing aisles
Of babies as they pushed their cart along.
Adoption rhetoric doesn't allow for a story
Of our birth, a connection to humanity.
No wonder so many of us felt we were aliens…
Being *chosen* by your adopters is nothing
compared with being *'UN-chosen'*
by your own mother,
which, despite the circumstances,
is how most of us feel."
--Julie, adoptee, *"Adoption Insights"*

BETTER TO KNOW

"It's better to know and be disappointed
than to never know and always wonder."
--(*"AwakeningPeople.com"*)

NO "GOOD" LIE

"There's a valid biological explanation
why all cultures, past and present,
hoist honesty to the top of the moral totem pole.
Those who lie to us put us in jeopardy.
We can protect ourselves from an assault
but not from an undiscovered lie."
--Attorney Gerry Spence
("How To Argue and Win Everytime")

ADOPTION MYTH #3:
"They'll get over it."

"Adoptees are expected to *'get over it.'*
I know now that we never get over great losses;
we absorb them, and they carve us into
different, yet often kinder, creatures."
--Unknown

THEY WERE WRONG

"Society said that biology didn't matter...
that Nurture was more important than Nature.
They were wrong.
It can bind families in more ways
That the brain can imagine.
And through my heart pumps the blood
Of my ancestors,
Which holds a connection
That cannot be replaced."
--Emm Paul *("Bastard Nation,"* 7-11-18)

BIOLOGICAL RELATIONSHIPS

"I lost the opportunity to know
what a natural, biological relationship is like
with a mother & father, brothers & sisters,
aunts & uncles & grandparents.
Observing natural families
makes me think it must be
such a beautiful thing to experience."
--A.B., Facebook (*Adoption Trauma*)

AMENDED IDENTITY

"The fact that one was adopted
does not solely define that person;
however, its ramifications
weave throughout one's identity,
often impacting relationships and choices
and often remaining a piece of identity
that is deeply personal
and one that is contemplated,
understood and processed,
and (re)understood
and (re)processed
again and again
as one ages."
--Tara Vanderwoude

MISSING LINK

"In the empty genetic mirror
the adoptee
stands alone."
--Claudia Corrigan D'Arcy, birth mother
(*"Musings of the Lame"*)

FRACTURED IDENTITY

"In the Old Testament, the phrase
"I will blot out their names"
is a more powerful threat
than even physical death."
--Dr. Rollo May (*"Man's Search for Himself"*)

A COMPLETE PERSON

"Fact: The Ellis Island Immigrant Web-site
had 8-million visitors in its first 8 hours.
I believe my research has
made me a more complete person."
--Elizabeth Bernstein, columnist,
Wall Street Journal, MSNBC-TV, 6/15/01

THE PERSON I WAS MEANT TO BE

"Were I to choose another's place
Select some famed one's state of grace
I'd be a farmer, planting seeds
And grow my undeveloped deeds.
I'd till the furrows of past years,
Tear out the choking weeds of fear,
And cultivate, for all to see
The unrealized potential Me.
No other's lot I seek to claim
No other's fortune or her fame,
Nor princess crown, nor movie screen,
For in my yard the grass is green.
I'll find no feast on others' shelf,
But nourish within myself,
Pluck from the branches of my tree
The person I was meant to be.
They look around but not within,
Who seek to don another's skin,
While I, my quest shall be to find
The Future Me I left behind."
--Rhonda Israelove

THE JOURNEY OF THE ADOPTED SELF

"Betwixt and between,
adopted "child" never grows up.
Birth certificate sealed;
secrecy and adoption go together,
secrecy the "magic broom."
Secrecy shapes and constricts,
in psychological misery.
Anger cannot be disguised,
helplessness, guilt.
Alienated, unreal, invisible, unborn,
adoption ghosts hovering.
Search for identity, *"Who am I?"*
Endless search for meaning in this strange fate,
abandonment defines experience.
Paste on images to form a self.
We carry ourselves, dead bodies, for lifetimes.
Broken narratives, lost stories,
disconnected from the human race;
sacred stories denied.
Kill the "birth" family, oversimplify,
mourning denied.
Cosmic loneliness, cut off from the
narrative point of origin,' buried treasure.
Sudden, unexpected, abnormal experience
equals psychological trauma.
Survive in numb, artificial self, dissociate,
disavow that forbidden self.
Empty, unentitled to life, selfless in desire to please,
escape defective, immoral 'birth' parents."
-Betty Jean Lifton, PhD, (1926-2010),
adoptee and counselor

LEGACY OF AN ADOPTED CHILD

"Once there were two women
Who did not know each other;
One you do not remember
The other you call "mother."
Two different lives,
Shaped to make yours one;
One became your guiding star,
The other became your sun.
The first gave you life,
And the second taught you to live it;
The first gave you a need for love,
And the second was there to give it.
One gave you nationality;
The other gave you a name.
One gave you the seed of talent
The other gave you an aim.
One gave you emotions;
The other calmed your fears.
One saw your first sweet smile,
The other dried your tears.
One gave you up;
It was all that she could do.
The other prayed for a child,
And was led straight to you."
-Author Unknown

THE FACE IN THE MIRROR

"....my reflection stares back and tells nothing,
no secrets revealed.
The things it seems I should know,
'the suffered anguish,
a memory of almost....
my mother's hair....
the eyes of my father
seen but not remembered,
I am an echo of the past,
a moment in time between two people,
an embrace, held for all time,
in all that is left,
me...."
--Victoria Santiago, adoptee ("*Identity*")

WHO?

"Adopted kids 'take after' their first parents,
not their adoptive parents."
--Robert Plomin, Behavioral Geneticist,
"*Birth Mother Forum,*"
Kings College, London, 1-4-19

NATURE v. NURTURE

"Each day of our lives, we make deposits
in the memory banks of our children"
--Charles R. Swindell

HEREDITY OR ENVIRONMENT?

"And now you ask me,
Through your tears,
The age-old question,
Through the years.
Heredity or environment,
Which are you the product of?
Neither, my darling, neither,
Just two different kinds of love."
--Author Unknown

THE GOOD ADOPTEE

"Superman was adopted.
But who can live up to Superman?"
-Unknown

THE BAD ADOPTEE

"How close to the edge can you go
before you are pulled over the edge?
The forbidden self, *"Bad adoptee,"*
transcends, unembodied, can't be trapped.
Return to the ghost kingdom,
to young mother, happy daddy,
picnic on a blanket with baby,
in a parallel universe,
where their marriage worked."
--Marybeth Budd, adoptee (*"Lizzie's Wishes"*)

A BETTER LIFE

"A 'better life' via adoption'
is what no social worker
can predict nor guarantee."
-Lori Carangelo, birth mother.
Founder, Americans For Open Records-AmFOR

WHY SEARCH?

"Fact: The Ellis Island Immigrant Web-site
had 8-million visitors in its first 8 hours.
The average person spends $700 annually on
genealogy.
I believe my research has
made me a more complete person."
--Elizabeth Bernstein, columnist,
Wall Street Journal, on MSNBC-TV, 6/15/01

WHAT IF

"I'd rather live a life of 'Oh wells'
than a life of 'what ifs.'"
--Marilyn Monroe

A GOOD TIME TO SEARCH

"If we wait until we're ready,
we'll be waiting the rest of our lives."
--Unknown Adoptee

FORGIVENESS

"Life is an adventure in forgiveness."
--Norman Cousins,
American Journalist (1915-1990)

HEALING

"One of the saddest things of all
is that so many adoptees and moms are afraid
to take the risk of healing
which is necessary to pursue one's dreams."
-Joe Soll, LCSW, adoptee
("Adoption Healing")

TURNING THE PAGE

"You can't start the next chapter
of your life
if you keep re-reading
the last one."
--*"Loveasagame.com"*

TRUTH

"All truths are easy to understand
once you discover them."
--Galileo

I AM ME

"Never waste your time trying to explain
who you are
to people who are committed to
misunderstanding you."
--rawforbeauty.com

BOGUS GENEALOGY

"In 4 generations,
half of Americans' ancestry will be bogus"
[due to sealed adoptions].
--Attorney Brice M. Clagett,
New England Historical Society

IMMEDIATE FAMILY

"The worldwide Mormon Family History Center
defines "Immediate family"
as one's grandparents, parents,
brothers, sisters, spouse, children and grandchildren;
in-laws are extended family —
as aunts, uncles and cousins."
--Abigail Van Buren, syndicated columnist,
"Dear Abby," Los Angeles Times, 5-30-92

SIX DEGREES OF SEPARATION

"Everyone on this planet
is separated by only six people....
but how to find the right six people..."
--John Guare (*"Six Degrees of Separation"*)

THEY COULD BE MY PEOPLE

"I was born to a woman I never knew
and raised by another who took in orphans.
I do not know my background, my lineage,
my biological or cultural heritage.
But when I meet someone new,
I treat them with respect.
For, after all, they could be my people."
--James Michener

TWO FAMILIES

"You don't have to choose between two families....
You just have a bigger family."
----Search Story, *San Francisco Chronicle*, 11-19-78

NOT A TRADE-OFF

"Children should never have to sacrifice
their biological identities
in order for a family
to love and care for them."
-Lynn Grubb

NEVER ASSUME

"Never assume that because a child was adopted
that their life is as wonderful as adoption
painted it out to be.
Many adoptees are grieving the loss
of their birth mother and family.
Those feelings don't go away
because a child is adopted."
-Facebook (*"I Am Adopted"*)

RISK

"And the day came when the risk
to remain closed as a bud became more painful
than the risk it took to blossom."
--Anais Nin

WHEN A SEARCH ENDS AT A GRAVE

"All the times I have suddenly realized
that my parents are dead,
even now, it still surprises me
to exist in the world
while that which made me
has ceased to exist."
--Nicole Krauss

GREATER LOSS

"Death is not the greatest loss.
The greatest loss is what dies inside us
while we live."
--Norman Cousins, American Journalist
(1915-1990)

GRIEF

"Grief is like the ocean;
it comes on waves
ebbing and flowing.
Sometimes the water is calm,
And sometimes it is overwhelming.
All we can do is learn to swim."
--Vicki Harrison

AFTER LOSS

"The reality is that you will grieve forever.
You will not 'get over' the loss
of loved ones;
You will learn to live with it."
You will heal and rebuild yourself
Around the loss you have suffered.
You will be whole again
But you will never be the same.
Nor should you be the same
Nor would you want to be."
--Elizabeth Kubler-Ross and David Kessler

WHEN LOVE HAS NO PLACE TO GO

"Grief, I've learned, is just love.
It's all the love you want to give but cannot.
All that unspent love gathers up
In the corners of your eyes,
The lump in your throat,
And in that hollow in your chest.
Grief is just love with no place to go."
--Anonymous

NO DEAD ENDS

"When one door is shut, another opens."
--Miguel De Cervantes

TOXIC PEOPLE

"To a toxic person,
disconnection is like a game.
They will continue to take themselves
Or whomever they can take away from you
as punishment,
and make you be the "bad person'
and them the victim."
--Corrine (*"The Pragmatic Parent"*)

A TOXIC FAMILY MEMBER

"A [toxic] family member will take advantage
of the fact that you are family –
a bond that is supposed to be enduring,
loving and respectful –
to manipulate and hurt you
because they know you will find it hard
to remove yourself
because you are family."
--Corrine ("*The Pragmatic Parent*")

PRIORITIES

"If it is important to you,
you will find a way.
If not,
You'll find an excuse."
--Unknown

I CARRY MY PARENT WITH ME

"I, who was borne away to become an orphan,
carry my parents with me.
So he groaned aloud in the ship
and hit his drum and laughed."
--Zora Neale Hurston ("*Jonah's Gourd*")

WORSE THAN DEATH

"In the Old Testament, the phrase
'*I will blot out their names*'
is a more powerful threat even than physical death."
--Dr. Rollo May ("*Man's Search for Himself*")

THE WHY AND HOW

"If he knows the 'why' for his existence,
he will be able to bear the 'how.'"
-Victor Frankel

THE WHAT

"What's in a name?
That which we call a rose
by any other name would smell as sweet."
--William Shakespeare ("*Romeo and Juliet*")

BRANDED BY LAW

"Without law, no little souls,
fresh from God, would be branded illegitimate
as soon as they reach the earth."
--Elbert Green Hubbard,
aka Fra Elbertus, Roycroft Press

WHY BASTARD?

"Why bastard? Wherefore base?
When my dimensions are as well compact,
My mind as generous, and my shape as true,
As honest madam's issue? Bastardy? base, base.
....Now gods, stand up for bastards!"
--William Shakespeare ("*King Lear*")

ILLEGITIMATE SON

"Ever since I can remember,
I was taught that Jesus was the *natural* son of Mary,
and the *adopted* son of God--
But that is wrong!
Jesus was the natural son of Mary,
the *step-son* of Joseph,
and the *illegitimate* son of God! Think about it!"
--Mrs. Colby Bell

NO ILLEGITIMATES

"There are no illegitimate children —
only illegitimate parents."
--Judge Leon R. Yanwich, U.S. District Court of
California, (quoting jurist O. McIntyre,
later paraphrased by U.S. Supreme Court Justice
William O. Douglas)

NO ANCESTRY

"Adopted people are not allowed ancestry
because it might upset somebody."
--Sandra K. Musser, birth mother, adoption activist

ADOPTED KIDS

"Adopted kids are such a pain –
You have to teach them how to look at you."
--Gilda Radner, Comedian (1946-1989),
(*"Saturday Night Live – SNL"*)

ON THE RECEIVING END

"The child is on the unkind receiving end
of his parents."
--L. Ron Hubbard (*"Dianetics"*)

NO SECRET

"My adoptive parents always told everyone
that we were adopted.
I can remember the kids in school asking
what was wrong with me
because my mother [must not have] wanted me
and [they] called me Little Orphan Annie."
--Anne Minigo Winslow
born Lily Marlene Tinger

VOICE FROM THE CABBAGE PATCH

"Don't treat adoptees
like cabbage patch dolls."
--Jo Glass, adoptee

ESCAPING THE CABBAGE PATCH

"Adoption was an Eighties thing.
People flying to Chile, all over the globe,
God knows where,
returning triumphantly with their BABY.
It was difficult, adventurous, expensive and generous.
It was trendy then.
People were into adopting bunches of babies
in all different flavors and colors
(Korean, Chinese, part-Indian was very popular;
Guatemalan - Guatemalan babies are very cute).
Adoption was a fad,
just like the Cabbage Patch dolls which fed the fad
to tens of thousands of pre-pubescent girl consumers."
-Joyce Williams (*"Baby Scam"*)

TRUE ORPHANS

"True orphans are those whose parents have died
and no one claims them.
Being labeled an '*economic* orphan' gives them
a one-way ticket to the world marketplace."
--Lori Carangelo, birth mother

TO LOVE AND BE LOVED

"To love and be loved
is to feel the sun from both sides."
--David Viscott, MD

FORGIVENESS

"Forgiveness comes as slowly as Winter turns into
summer, or longer....
It's a necessary emotional process, and it's befitting.
Our parents gave us life;
Without their ability to "let go" for whatever reason,
we would not be who we are today.
There has to be a reconciliation with ourselves,
our hurt and our rage.
It's a passive state we need to attain.
Passing through the pain leads to understanding.
Non-acceptance is to remain fixated.
All life eventually balances itself.
We must allow our lives to reflect healing."
--Georgianne Bone, adoptee
founder, "*New Life*" adoptee support group

INABILITY TO FORGIVE

"Emotional illness can be said to be caused by
the inability to forgive.
It isn't the trauma that causes the illness;
it's the repression of the trauma."
--John Bradshaw (*"Our Families, Ourselves"*)

DIGNITY

"The beginning and end of 'child psychology'
is that a child is a human being,
that he is entitled to his dignity
and self-determination."
--L. Ron Hubbard (*"Dianetics"*)

CLOSED ADOPTION

"Closed adoption is institutionalized denial."
--Nancy Murray, LCSW
(Adoption Placement Supervisor,
"The Whole Family")

MALPRACTICE

"Closed adoption is malpractice."
--Reuben Pannor, MSW, LCSW

WHO AM I?

"Until I hold my original birth certificate
in my hand,
I can only be sure of who I'm *not*,
Not who I *am*."
--Robert McCullough, adult adoptee

POLITICS

"Politics, rather than an understanding
of children's needs,
often dictate decisions about a child's placement."
--Eileen T. Brazelton, pediatric physician, and
Barry T. Brazelton, MD
(*"A Psychiatrist Comments"*)

PSYCHIATRY

"Psychiatry is a form of social engineering."
--Jean Paton, MA, MSW, adoptee (1908-2002)
(founder in 1953 of *The Open Records Movement,* and
Anti-Adoption Movement in the United States)

FOREVER FAMILY, FOREVER CHILD

"Not to have knowledge of what happened
before you were born
is to be condemned
to live forever as a child."
-Cicero (c.106-43 BC)

DEPRESSION

"Depression is really anger against yourself."
--Art Buchwald

ONE BIG HAPPY FAMILY

"When you're surrounded by all these people,
it can be lonelier than when you're by yourself.
You can be in a huge crowd,
But if you don't' feel like you can trust anyone
Or talk to anybody,
You feel like you're really alone."
--Fiona Apple

DONOR OFFSPRING

"I'm not a 'treatment,'
I'm a person…
…And those records belong to me."
--Olivia Pratten, journalist,
("*Donor Conceived*")

2.
BIRTH
MOTHERS

LOSS

"The horrors of war
pale against the loss of a child."
-Joe Soll, LCSW, adoptee
(paraphrasing Anna Freud)

ADOPTION MYTH # 4
"Adoptions decrease abortions."

"'Adoption lessens abortions' …
is statistically untrue…
Adoption aborts the mother."
--Author Unknown
(*"The Adoption & Donor Conception Factbook"*)

UNPLANNED PREGNANCY

"Death, taxes and childbirth!
There's never a convenient time
for any of these."
--Margaret Mitchell, (*"Gone With The Wind"*)

ADOPTION'S BUZZ WORDS

"Being a mother is a noble status, right?
So why does it change
when you put "unwed" or "welfare" in front of it?"
--Gloria Steinem, founder, Feminist Party,
(*"The Verbal Karate of Florynce R. Kennedy,"*
MS Magazine)

STILL A MOTHER

"Some mothers get to hold and raise their children.
Others only get to weep
over babies they loved and lost –
But remember, having empty arms makes them
no less a mother."
--*"Saying Goodbye.org"*

THE WORD "MOTHER"

"'Mother' can be a very loaded word.
You may experience anything
from pleasure to grief to anger to guilt to nothing.
The first thing to remember is that
whatever experience you had
was triggered by a word."
--Author Unknown

ADOPTION MYTH # 5
"As if it never happened."
"Ever had a memory
that sneaks out of your eye
and rolls down your check?"
--*"Soul Searchers"*

"GIFT" OF ADOPTION?

"Adoption – the 'gift' that keeps on taking."
--Michelle Beecher, birth mother

TIME

"It's not a moment in time –
A grieving [birth mother] is going to laugh again
And smile again.
Yes, they have to move forward.
But that doesn't mean they'd moved on."
--Unknown

COLLUSION

"The young woman with poor self-esteem
and low assertiveness
might take decades or forever
to drop her denial
and collusion with the beliefs
pedaled by the [adoption] agency."
--Geoff Rickarby, MB BS, New South Wales Parliament
(*"Committee on Past Adoption Practices"*)

A MOTHER'S LOVE

"Had I loved him any less – one ounce less –
he would be with me now!
My love for him was the only thing
That could enable me to break my own heart."
--Tamra Hyde

BIRTH MOTHER

"They took you to another home
Intending to forever separate us;
For a moment, again our hearts met.
Then you moved on.
Whether in this life or the next,
We will meet again, my child,
And in that place,
Again love will come home."
--Lori Carangelo ("*Treasures To Discover*,"
International Library of Poetry, 2000)

SPECIAL DELIVERY

"No mother goes into a delivery room
and delivers an orphan."
--Danina Concetta Italiano
("*Lost Generations*")

TIES THAT BIND

"Children and mothers
never truly part,
bound together
by the beating of one another's heart."
--Charlotte Gray

WAS IT EVEN A DECISION?

"I know I made the right decision.
But my brain knowing doesn't stop
My heart from wondering."
--Ilene, birth mother

PRE-BIRTH MATCHING

"Pre-birth matching is when
hopeful adoptive parents
court an expectant mother
in an attempt to woo her
into giving her baby to them."
-(*Musings of a Birthmom*)

INVOLUNTARY RELINQUISHMENT

"'Voluntary' relinquishment is a myth."
--Hal Aigner, adoptee and journalist,
San Francisco Chronicle

PLAYING GOD

"Playing God is God's job –
not agency workers.'"
--Linda Arteman-Wilshusen,
birth parent and adoptive parent

CONTRACTS

"She signed a piece of paper, didn't she?
Well, so did slave sellers;
so did indentured servants
who virtually sold themselves into slavery
for a term of years;
so did long-ago impoverished parents
who sold their daughters into brothels.
And every day in this country,
contracts are entered into for drug deals,
murders for hire,
arson, insurance scams, illegal gambling,
and, yes, child selling
....A deal is a deal, right Your Honor?"
-Richard H. Rosichan (*"Baby M,"* a surrogacy case,
quoting Judge Sorkow *"A Deal is a Deal,"*
New York Times, 4-4-87)

WHEN A DEAL IS NOT A DEAL

"What the Supreme Court really did was rule that
a human soul is more important than a contract,
and that Judge Sorkow's philosophy that
'a deal is a deal' is wrong
when the deal involves the selling of a human being.
Seven-to-zero wrong.
--A.M. Rosenthal (*"Baby M,"*
surrogacy case, Washington Post, 2-20-87)

THE PAST IS GONE

"Don't cry, it's just your whole life changing
the past is gone
the future not yet formed
and this fleeting you right now
poised tiptoe at the edge of the bluff
leaning forward, spreading your wings
ready to pause a moment
don't forget you,
suddenly this essential you
it is not the leap
it is the courage
it is the will
remember your will
remember your love
remember your courage
remember your intense craving for life
daring to give and get trust and love
don't forget
you are more than what you do
remember you
now jump!"
--Jacke, birth mother

SINGLE MOM

"Single mom confession:
'People think my child was a mistake.
He wasn't. His father was.'"
--Whisper

FIRST BIRTH MOTHER

"And when she could no longer hide him,
she took him an ark of bulrushes,
and daubed it with slime and with pitch,
and put the child therein;
and she laid it in the flags by the river's brink."
--*"Exodus 2:3," The Bible*

SEPARATION

"Probably the most stressful and anxiety-provoking act
in human existence is the separation of a woman
from her newborn infant.
The response to this, which humans share
with most of the animal kingdom, is an
overwhelming combination of panic, rage, distress.
Who can dare judge the psychological acts
and responses
of a woman put to such a test?
In the present-day United States,
what psychologist can claim to have
experience with women subject to that experience?"
--A.P. Rushkin, MD, letter to the editor,
New York Times, 4-20-87

NO EX'S

"There are ex-husbands and ex-wives but there are
no ex-moms, ex-dads or ex-children."
-Joe Soll, LCSW, adoptee
(*"Adoption Healing"*)

TRUTH

"The only thing that lives on is truth;
It passes in secret from one heat to another;
It passes in mother's milk to her child."
--The Egyptians

CHILDREN AS STRANGERS

"Mamas don't let your babies grow up to be strangers."
--Jess DelBalzo, founder,
"Adoption: Legalized Lies"

FROM GIRL TO MOTHER

"When a girl is under 21, she's protected by law;
When she's over 65, she's protected by Nature;
Anything in between is fair game."
--Cary Grant (*"Operation Petticoat"*)

A PRISON WITHOUT BARS

"My son was born a miracle, a life that God created.
But I was required to give away my child long awaited.
No gray stone walls, no steel barred cell
could have imprisoned me so well
as the iron grip of grinding grief
that keeps me locked in pain."
--Author Unknown

LIZZIE'S WISHES

"I want to be there
for the whole trip, to see you grow up
and marry, have children of your own.
I want to bake your favorite pies,
sew your dresses and shirts,
read you my favorite books,
see your teenaged years.
I want to tell you stories
of your grandparents, while peeling
and slicing apples, rolling out the dough,
sprinkling cinnamon, sugar and raisins....
....I want to sit on the front porch
and watch you chase fireflies,
tuck you into bed each night
with prayer and bedtime stories.
Instead I watch the stars
snow falls on my quilt.
Instead I give up wishing
all earthly desire subsides,
with it, pain, anguish, despair.
Too soon I join the stars,
watch my daughter bake pies,
read to my grandchildren,
pass on my wishes with my life."
--Marybeth Budd, adoptee
(*"Lizzie's Wishes"*)

66

THEY SAID

"they said i had to go to a home for unwed mothers
they never asked me what i wanted to do;
they said my baby should have a mother and a father;
they never gave me a choice to help me see it through;
they said the line in my belly would disappear;
they never mentioned the wound in my heart;
they said go on with your life
and pretend it didn't happen;
they never told me i would grieve
all the years we're apart;
they said i should be happy now that i'm free;
they never admit my flesh and blood
has been amputated from me;
they said i could get married,
other children would call me mother;
they never said one person does not replace another;
they said why, she has a good life;
they never listen to how the pain of not knowing
cuts like a knife;
they aid it's against the law to search and find her
they never knew this was my heart's desire
they said she's still young
and has other things on her mind;
they say you're getting older,
you've been waiting a long time;
they said when she has children,
she'll want to know me;
they never concede i missed sharing her life,
she never sat on my knee
they said if i loved my baby i'd sign the paper
and leave that day;
she said, don't tell me you love me –
you gave me away."
--Sheila Ganz, birth mother
founder, *"Bay Area Birthmothers Association"*

LITTLE DID YOU KNOW, MAYBE

"Little did you know
....hoping for the best
when you gave that baby away
....let God provide
how perfect a creature
...maybe they'll adopt her
she can grow up
...I'll get on
poisoned by grief
...with my life
and anger.
Not for one second
...maybe
children escape
...break the spell
of parents' sins
...maybe
a vast difference
...she'll have
between two parents
...a better
life
…or none."
--Marybeth Budd, adoptee,
(*"Lizzie's Wishes"*)

I'LL SEE YOU THERE

"I keep you in my prayers, and always will....
Till the day you die.
And when the time comes,
that you and I should leave this world
and enter the next,
I will see you there and we will both be free."
--Sandra Wilson, birth mother

ONLY A LOVE SONG

"I know there is a reason
That we have been growing apart
But choosing to love you forever
I've chosen for growth in my heart
This is only a love song, my daughter
If it be as it is now
That you must be hidden from view
I pray that these loving strains
Find a way to you
If I could see you growing
I'd only be happier then
And how can I tell you I love you
If I cannot see you again
I want your heart to blossom
I pray that your spirit accept
The love that creation will show you
Much more love will come to you yet
I have left my life open
If you want to see me again
I'm hoping that one day I'll see you
And praying we'll grow as true friends."
--Imelda Buckley ("*Only A Love Song*")

A MOTHER'S LOVE

"A mother's love for her child
is like nothing else in the world.
It knows no law, no pity.
It dares all things.
And crashes down remorselessly
All that stands in its path."
--Agatha Christie

DREAMS

"I dream of you all day
Think of you while I sleep....
Thoughts of you are always with me....
Dreaming of the day that we meet.
I wonder about the little things,
What color are your eyes?
What makes you smile?
What makes you cry?
Who do you call mommy?
And is she good to you?
I wonder do you need me....
As much as I need you?
I promise you I'm looking,
And one day soon we'll meet
Until then she'll take care of you....
And I'll see you in my dreams."
--Anonymous birth mother
(*"Dreams"*)

FROM LOSS TO ANGER

"The horrors of war pale
beside a mother who has lost her child."
--Anna Freud, psychologist,
daughter of Sigmund Freud

A MOTHER'S PAIN

"Mental pain is less dramatic than physical pain,
but it is more common and more hard to bear.
The frequent attempts to conceal mental pain
increases the burdens.
It is easier to say 'My tooth is aching'
Than to say 'My heart is breaking.'"
--C.S. Lewis, (*"The Problem of Pain"*)

REUNION OF A MOTHER AND SON

"Giving you up wasn't easy to do,
All I wanted was the best for you.
The tears fell as I gave you away,
My heart was breaking and the pain would stay.
You have always been close to me,
Not in person, but in my heart you'd be.
As the days turned into years,
I couldn't be there to calm your fears.
You may not realize what you've done for me,
My heart is healing as it should be.
Thank you for all of your love,
I also thank the Good Lord above.
Just remember I'm here for you,
Thank you, Paul, I love you a lot."
--Annette McCloud-Dowl

POST-REUNION, A ROCKY ROAD

"Every time you go… away…
you take a piece of me… with you…"
--original song by Daryll Hall and John Otis, 1980

REJECTION

"Love felt by the [birth] parent
does not automatically translate
into love experienced by the [adopted] child."
--Dr. Gabor Matè

TIME LIMIT

"The only people who think
there is a time limit on grief
have never lost a piece of their heart.
--healthylifeharbinger.wordpress.com

SURROGATES

"Sarah suggested that Abraham impregnate Hagar
in order 'that I may obtain children by her,'
but Hagar was a slave.
What's modern about this story is that,
once pregnant,
Hagar, like Marybeth Whitehead,
seemed to think the child was hers....
no matter what anyone said...."
--Katha Pollitt (*"The Nation"*)

3.
BIRTH
FATHERS

ADOPTION MYTH #6
"Birth fathers have no rights or interest ."
"We can't keep telling fathers
to have equal responsibility
and not give them equal rights."
-Pinterest.com

STILL A FATHER

"Just as a birth mother is no less a mother
because she chooses to place her child,
a birth father is still the child's father as well.
While there are adoptions that occur
where one or both birth parents are not involved,
or the father was never notified of an adoption,
or they need to have limited rights for safety reasons,
many times both birth parents are placing
out of a love for their child
and place out of necessity.
Fathers should not be treated as 'second class'
when it comes to their importance
to the adoption process
or their importance to their children,
simply because that 's what society
has always demanded.
It is time for change in the rights of fathers
who want the right to be heard
and who love their children."
–Lita Jordan

ALIENATION, THEN ADOPTION

"They burned the bridge,
then ask why I don't visit."
--Lindy Thiel
(*"Broken Relationships"*)

WITHOUT A FATHER

"A child without a father
is like a house without a roof."
-Chinese proverb

NOT READY

"Why are men reluctant to be fathers?
They aren't through being children."
-Cindy Garner

A SON'S BEST INTEREST

"According to most studies of the subject
boys who grow up without a father
grow up at a disadvantage."
-Clayton Lessor, MA, LPC

FATHERLESS,
NOT ILLEGITIMATE

"The child is different
not because he is illegitimate,
but because he is fatherless
and he is going to miss a father
in the same way that any child
who loses a father early
through death or separation, misses him."
--Lena Jeger,
(*"Illegitimate Children and Their Parents"*)

SOMETHING TO DO WITH ME

"When I was a kid,
I was told that I had a biological father,
but that he didn't have much importance.
I had an adoptive father who was present,
who loved me, who was up to the task.
And he was.
So, I didn't question that story, until I was thirty-two,
and suddenly realized that I was curious,
that he did have something to do with me."
--Melissa Febos

NO EXPERIENCE NEEDED

"The nature of impending fatherhood is that
you are doing something you're unqualified to do,
and then you become qualified while doing it."
--John Green

TRY

"You will find that if you really try to be a father,
your child will meet you halfway."
-Unknown

WHAT SONS ARE FOR

"Sons are born
to make their fathers better men."
-Mekal Shane

COMPLETION

"A man is not complete
until he has seen the baby he has made."
--Sammy Davis Jr.

BECOMING A MAN

"Never is a man more of a man
than when he is the father of a newborn."
--Matthew McConaghey

CONNECTING

"Having a staring contest with his newborn
is one of the weirdest things you he ever do.
And it is highly recommended."
--Ross McCamman

MORE THAN A TITLE

"'Father' is the noblest title a man can be given.
It is more than a biological role.
It signifies a patriarch, a leader, and exemplar,
A confident, a teacher, a hero, a friend."
--Robert L. Blackman

EXPECTATIONS

"A father is a man who expects his son
to be as good a man as he meant to be."
--Frank A. Clark

PARENTHOOD

"We don't lose ourselves in parenthood;
we find parts of ourselves
we never knew existed."
-L.R. Knost

BEING THERE

"A good father is a man who supports his children
even when he has no money."
--Coolnsmart.com

A "REAL" FATHER

"I have obviously spent some time
calculating the expense of being a father.
And the fact is, a 'real' father doesn't do
that kind of math."
-Craig D. Lounsbrough

PERSPECTIVE

"A truly rich man
is one whose children
run into his arms
when his hands are empty."
--Unknown

DISCOVERY

"There are places in the heart
you don't even know exist
until you have a child."
--Ann Lamont

DAD

"Dad – a son's first hero,
a daughter's first love."
--Quotes99.com

EASIER

"It is easier for a father to have children
than for children to have a 'real' father."
--Pope John XXIII

WHY GOD IS A FATHER

"'I always wondered why God
was supposed to be a father,' she whispered.
Fathers always want you to measure up to something;
Mothers are the ones who love you unconditionally."
-Jodi Picoult

A FATHER'S LOVE

"A father's love is no less than a mother's."
-Facebook.com/PAPAfightpas

MEANING

"No man can possibly know what life means,
what the world means,
what anything means,
until he has a child and loves it."
--Lafcaioltearn

PROTECTOR

"I cannot think of any need in childhood
as strong as the need for a father's protection."
--Sigmund Freud

NECESSITY BY ACCIDENT

"Fathers are biological necessities,
but social accidents."
--Margaret Mead

WHEN DAD'S A SPERM DONOR

"Anonymous sperm donors
have no unlimited right to privacy.'
--Ruling in Donor Offspring lawsuit,
San Francisco, AP, 8-24-00

ONLY HIM

"I knew that I could never find my father
in any other man who came into my life
because it was a void in my life
that could only be filled by him."
--Halle Berry

A WISE FATHER

"It is a wise father that knows his own child."
-William Shakespeare
(*"The Merchant of Venice"*)

REMEMBERING HIM

"It doesn't matter who my father was;
it matters who I remember he was."
--Anne Sexton

DADDY SIGNED

"Agencies and lawyers arrange;
Daddy signs if mom disappears.
Orphaned or not, find them a home.
Parents rearrange, interchange.
Tunnels of time, travel back and forth.
Institutions decide human affairs.
On with your life or repeat parents' mistakes,
Not knowing nightmares;
blood sucking deception sealed."
--Marybeth Budd, adoptee
(*"Lizzie's Wishes"*)

4.
BIRTH
SIBLINGS

"DUDE! I'm joking. *You're* not adopted

SEPARATED SIBS

"I was supposed to understand
my brother would have a better life
without me."
-Kept Sibling (*mythmisgivings*)

MISSING IN ADOPTION

"You realize how much
you truly miss someone
when something happens,
good or bad,
and the only person
you want to tell it to
is the person who isn't there."
--Unknown

SIBLING SEARCH

"A sibling may be the keeper
of one's identity,
the only person with the keys
to one's unfettered, more fundamental self."
--Marian Sandmaier

SHARED ROOTS

"Like branches of a tree
we grow in different directions
yet our roots remain as one.
Each of our lives will always be
A special part of the other's."
--"*SayingInmages.com*"

WHY SIBS RELATE

"Siblings will take different paths
and life may separate them,
but they will be forever bonded
by having begun their journey
in the same boat."
--Facebook post ("*Zen to Zany*")

NOT MEMORIES

"It's not the memories in my head
that drive me crazy.
It is the new moments created without you
that push me over the edge."
--Sanara ("*Heavensbook Angels*")

SEPARATED LATER

"Siblings share more than parents.
They share magical moments
That time can never erase."
--Facebook post (*"Zen to Zany"*)

TWINS

"Twins are two separate beings
conjoined at the heart."
--Kamand Kojowri

TWIN CONNECTION

"Twins share the womb' chemistry and
endure many fateful 'slings and arrows' together.
The fabled connection between twins
Is true in my case."
--Gregory Benford

MY TWIN, ANOTHER VERSION OF ME

"I guess because twins have this mystique …
and triplets…
…I think the normal sibling connection
potentially can be powerful,
…and there's the idea that it's even more powerful.
It really is.
Not just someone *like* me
But another version of me."
--Curtis Sittenfeld

SAME DNA

"It's a twin type of telepathy.
My sister and I, we share the same DNA,
So on paper, we're the same person.
I knew she was pregnant, like right away –
It's so crazy - but I asked her.
And she said yes."
--Tia Mowry

TRIPLETS

"It was cruel; it was wrong."
--David Kellman, a triplet separated at birth
from his brothers ,
Bobby Shafran and Eddie Galland
(*"Three Identical Strangers,"* Sundance Films)

DISAPPEARANCE BY ADOPTION

"Not only had my brother disappeared, but –
and bear with me now –
a part of my very being had gone with him.
Stories about us could,
from then on,
be told from only one perspective –
Memories could be told but not shared."
--John Corey Whaley
(*"Where Things Come Back"*)

GONE

"Never thought I would lose you
But here I am standing alone
Without you by my side,
We're sisters for life,
We promised,
But now you're gone,
I don't know what to do
Without you."
--Adriana (*"Love You"*)

ALWAYS PART OF YOU

"Sisters and brothers are the truest,
purest form of love, family and friendship,
knowing when to hold you and
when to challenge you,
but always being part of you."
--Carol Ann Albright Eastman

SIBLING REUNION

"We were meant to be joined by blood,
but we chose to be joined by love."
-Lvze.com

RECONNECTING

"A sibling is a friend given by Nature."
--Jean Baptiste Legouve

DISCOVERING A BROTHER

"Which of us has known his brother?
Which of us has looked into his father's heart?
Which of us has not remained forever prison-bent?
Which of us is not forever a stranger and alone?"
--Thomas Wolfe
(*"The Web and the Rock"*)

MY "REAL" BROTHER

"Being his 'real' brother,
I could feel I live in his shadow
But I never have and do not now.
I live in his glow."
--Michael Morpurgo

LONG LOST BROTHER

"To my brother:
You're the best friend
I was born to have."
--Unknown

BROTHERS AND SISTERS

"Brothers and sisters
can say things to each other
that no one else can"
--Gregory E. Lang

HOW IRONIC

"I smile because you're my brother,
and I laugh
because there's nothing you can do about it."
-Unknown

ACCEPTANCE

"One a brother, always a brother,
no matter the distance,
no matter the differences,
and no matter the issue."
-Byron Pulsifer

SIBS HAPPEN

"Sisters and brothers just happen;
we don't get to choose them;
but they become one of our
most cherished relationships."
-Wes Adamson

BAD BROTHER

"A bad brother
is far better than no brother."
-Swahili proverb

COMFORT OF A BROTHER

"Brothers don't necessarily have to say anything
to each other –
they can sit in a room and be together
and just be completely comfortable
with each other."
--Leonardo DiCaprio, American actor

SISTERS

"In the cookies of life,
sisters are the chocolate chips."
--Anonymous

LOVE OF A SISTER

"I love you, Sis.
And I promise you this.
No matter who enters your life,
I will love you more than any of them."
--Unknown

SISTERS KNOW

"A sister always knows
when to listen and when to talk,
when to laugh and when to cry."
--Anonymous

CLOSENESS OF SISTERS

"My sister and I are so close
that we often finish each other's sentences
and often wonder whose memories
belong to whom."
--Shannon Celebi

A "REAL" SISTER

"You are a dream I never dared dream
You are the wish I could not say
You are the make-believe friend
who shared my lonely room
Shared so many tea parties
So many secrets I told you
Never in my little girl heart
Could I have imagined
You were real
You were wishing the same wishes
You were dreaming the same dreams
You were having the same tea party
You told me your secrets
Now we have that special love
That love that only sisters know
The love was just a silent
Wish kept deep in our little girl hearts....
The love of a sister."
--Author Unknown

MORE

"Having lots of siblings
is like having built-in best friends."
--Kim Kardashian

COMPARING

"Comparison's a death knell to sibling harmony."
-Elizabeth Fishnel

SIBLING POWER

"Children of the same family,
the same blood,
with the same first associations and habits,
have some means of enjoyment
in their power,
which no subsequent connections can supply."
--Jane Austen (*"Mansfield Park"*)

FREEDOM OF SISTERS

"There's a special kind of freedom
sisters enjoy –
freedom to share innermost thoughts,
to ask a favor,
to show their true feelings."
--Anonymous

THE GREATEST GIFT

"The greatest gift our parents ever gave us
was each other."
--Unknown

BE NICE

"Be nice to your siblings;
they're your best link to your past
and the most likely to stay with you in the future."
--Baz Lurhmann

SIBLING PERSPECTIVE

"A sibling is the lens
through which you see your childhood."
-bayart.org

SIBLING RELATIONSHIPS

"Sibling relationships... outlast marriages,
survive the death of parents,
resurface after quarrels
that would sink any friendship.
The flourish in a thousand incarnations
of closeness and distance,
warmth, loyalty and distrust."
--Erica E. Goode

CLOSE RELATIONSHIP

"When you're in a relationship
and it's good,
even if nothing else in your life is right,
you feel like you're whole world is complete."
--hpLyrikz.com

BUT NOT TOO CLOSE

"Caligula and his younger sister, Drusilla,
had an incestuous relationship
'because no one else loved them.'"
--The History Channel, 2-7-10

[Note: In most states, siblings, whether by birth or adoption, cannot legally marry. The assumed reason that even non-biologically related adoptive sibs are prohibited from marrying is to prevent perceived 'family chaos.' But also, according to Winona Durbin (former social worker, Riverside County, CA), in regions where there is a high concentration of adoption placements of separated siblings, there are reports of incestuous marriages between siblings *unaware* of their biological relationships.

[But that doesn't seem to bother lawmakers who favor sealed adoptions.]

5.
ADOPTIVE
MOTHERS

CHOOSING MOTHERHOOD

"I believe the choice to become a mother
is the choice to become one of the greatest
spiritual leaders there is."
--Oprah Winfrey

HAYLEY

"Your hair, that tickles my nose,
is a different color than mine,
and your chin, quivering when you cry,
may look like someone else,
and though you don't have my eyes,
you capture me with a glance,
because I see, thee deep inside,
a part of me: you have my heart."
--James M. Thompson (*"Hayley"*)

'REAL' PARENT

"'Real' Parent (a noun):
Any Parent who is not imaginary."
--Adoption.com

INFERTILITY

"Adoption is not a cure for infertility."
-Joe Soll, LCSW, adoptee
(*"Adoption Healing"*)

ADOPTION MYTH #7
"An adopted child is a gift from God."

"Where does the right of ownership come from?
Is it a divine right? Does it come from God?
It is merely a rule of man, is it not?"
--Attorney Gerry Spence
(*"How To Argue and Win Every Time"*)

ADOPTION MYTH #8:
"The 'as born to' myth."

"Whoever rears an orphan,
it is as though he has brought him into the world."
-The Talmud
[Note: probably the origin of the modern
"as born to" myth when it had to do with
a man's need of a male heir]

ACKNOLWEDGEMENT

"Our greatest joy… is her greatest pain."
--Unknown, Adoption Network Law Center

NOT FORGOTTEN

"A child born to another woman calls me mom.
The depth of the tragedy
and the magnitude of the privilege
are not lost on me."
--Jody Landers, adoptive mother

WHY SEALED?

"Neither society nor the adopter
who holds the child in her arms
wants to confront the agony
of the mother from whose arms
that same child was taken."
--Margaret McDonald Lawrence,
Adoption.com

PERSPECTIVE

"He's mine in a way that he will never be hers,
yet he's hers in a way he will never be mine;
and so, together,
we are motherhood."
--Desha Wood

ROLES

"Stepparents [or adoptive parents] are not around
to replace biological parents,
rather to augment a child's life experience."
--Azriel Johnson

UNDERSTANDING

"I want adoption to be *part* of my child's story
but I don't want it to be his/her only story."
--Jen (*"Open Adoption/Open Heart*)

MORE THAN LOVE

"Some adoptive parents find
love alone isn't the answer."
-("*Getting a Hold on Rage*,"
Detroit Free Press, 6-25-95)

BELONGING

"When adopters say 'I don't know why my kid lies,'
I say 'He's one of society's biggest lies:
You belong in this family.'"
--Nancy Verrier, MA, MFT, Adopter
(*"Birth Scene-A Different King of Relationship:
Thoughts on Adoption"*)

NOT YOUR CHILDREN

"Your children are not your children.
They are the sons and daughters
of life's longing for itself.
They come through you but not from you.
And though they are with you,
yet they belong not to you.
You may give them your love but not your thoughts,
For they have their own thoughts.
You may house their bodies but not their souls,
For their souls dwell in the house of tomorrow,
which you cannot visit, not even in your dreams.
You may strive to be like them,
but seek not to make them like you."
--Kahil Gibran

CUSTODIAL PARENTS

"Had I to do it over again,
I would have opted for Legal Guardianship
or remained a foster parent,
rather than burden
our adopted daughter and us
with all the inequities
that the adoption system imposed on us.
I wish we could call adoptive parents
'custodial parents'
which I think is more correct.
We have custody of the child
and only that."
--Sheila Grove, adoptive mom
(*"Adoption Uncensored,"* page 249)

CHILDREN ARE INDIVIDUALS

"Children aren't coloring books;
you don't get to fill them in
with your favorite colors."
--Khaled Hasseini

MOST IMPORTANT VOICE

"You will hear many voices
on Adoption and Adoptees—
but none is more important
than that of your [adopted] child."
-Madeline Melcher, Adoption.net

OBJECTIVE

"Adoption is not about
finding children for families,
it's about finding families for children."
--Joyce Maguire Pavao

UNSELFISH LOVE

"One does not love one's children
just because they are one's children,
but because of the friendship formed
while raising them."
--Gabriel Garcia Marquez

EXPECTATIONS

"There is no formula
for making a stranger's child
live up to their adopter's expectations.
To a child, the burden of such expectations
translates as abuse."
--Jack Kresnak

HONORING THE BIRTH FAMILY

"When you honor the birth family
you honor the child.
When you don't honor the birth family,
The child believes something is
inherently wrong with him/her."
--ReciteThis.com

6.
ADOPTIVE
FATHERS

SOMEONE ELSE'S CHILDREN

"It takes a strong man
to accept someone else's children
and step up to the plate
another man left on the table."
--Your Daily Quotes (*"16quotes.com"*)

RESPECT FOR ADOPTIVE FATHERS

"I respect any man who can
raise a child he didn't make,
heal the heart he didn't break,
put some food on the plate,
not make the same mistake."
-pear.org, Instagram message

ADOPTIVE FATHER'S LOVE

"A real man loves another man's child
As he would his own.
Thank you for loving me."
-LoveThisPic.com

FATHER AND SON

"It's not flesh and blood but heart
which makes us father and son."
-Johann Friedrich von Schiller

KNOW THY FATHER

"I certainly knew my father.
He just didn't happen to be my biological father."
--Jack Nicholson, American actor

WHAT MAKES A FATHER

"…Any fool can have a child.
That doesn't make you a father.
It's the courage to raise a child
That makes you a father."
--President Barack Obama

PERFECT PARENT

"Fathering is not something perfect men do,
but something that perfects the man."
--Frank Pittman

GROWTH

"I realized at the start
that whether a child is biological or adopted,
one does not know all the ingredients in the package.
That is what growth is about.
A child is the slowest flower in the world,
opening petal by petal,
revealing the developing personality within."
-Robert Klose, adoptive father

DAD

"Of all the titles I've been privileged to have
'Dad' has always been the best."
--Ken Norton

STANDING TALL

"No man stands taller
than when he stoops to help a child."
--Abraham Lincoln

PROTECTOR

"He adopted the role of being a father
so that his child would have something
mythical and infinitely important:
a protector."
--Tom Wolfe

FATHERLY EXAMPLE

"Every father should remember
one day his son will follow his example,
not his advice."
--Charles Ketterling

LEGACY

"The best inheritance a parent can give his child
is a few minutes of his time each day."
--O.A. Battista

TRADING PLACES

"You spend the first half of your life
trying to make your parents proud of you;
Then you spend the second half of your life
trying to make your kids proud of you."
--Neil Simon, playwrite

HER DADDY

"The only man a girl can depend on
is her Daddy."
--Frenchy

FATHERS OF DAUGHTERS

"It is desirable for a man to take his son fishing;
but there is a special place in heaven
for the father who takes his daughter shopping."
--John Siner

ADOPTION MYTH #9:
"Sex with one's consenting adopted child is okay because they are not biologically related."

"It's incestuous even if it's not incest."
--FrancoisHerifi, psychology professor,
(commenting on the affair between
actor Woody Allen and Soon-Yi Previn,
Mia Farrow's daughter adopted from Korea)

6 THINGS TO SAY

"6 Things parents can say to kids playing sports:
Have fun,
play hard,
I love you,
Did you have fun?
I'm proud of you.
I love you."
--ee cards

SONS OF FATHERS

"For rarely are sons similar to their fathers;
most are worse,
and a few are better than their fathers."
--Homer (*"The Odyssey"*)

A COMMITMENT

"Adoption is commitment
that you enter into blindly,
but it is no different than
adding a child by birth.
It is essential that adoptive parents
are committed to making it work,
committed to parenting this child
for the rest of their lives,
and committed to parenting
through the tough stuff."
–Brooke Randolph

LGBQ AND TRANSGENDER ADOPTION

"Everyone is entitled to the same
human rights and equal protection.
But mixing adoption with other political issues
such as abortion and LGBQT parenthood
not only ignores rights of the child
and his/her biological family,
it is also often mis-communicated as a
'right to *adopt'*--
NO ONE has a '*right* to adopt' another's child."
--Lori Carangelo, birth mother,
(founder, *Americans For Open Records-AmFOR* - responding
to a 2011 mailing by Anthony Romero, American Civil
Liberties Union-ACLU Executive Director promoting
LGBQT "*right* to adopt"; see *"LGBT, ACLU and the 'Right'
To Adopt – A Third View"*- LoriCarangelo.com/gay.html;"
and "*AdoptionUncensored,*" p 278)

7.
ADOPTION
ACTIVISTS

A VOICE HEARD AROUND THE WORLD

"This is all wrong...How *DARE* you!" ...
"I have learned you are never too small
to make a difference."
--Greta Thunberg, age 16,
(Swedish Climate Activist addressing the
United Nations Climate Summit, 2019,
for failing to take action,
prompting Climate Strikes across 139 countries;
she was nominated for the Nobel Peace Prize)

ONE VOICE

"When the world is silent,
even one voice becomes powerful...
One child, one teacher, one book,
and one pen
can change the world."
--Malala Yousafzai, Nobel Prize Winner
(in a speech to the United Nations Youth Assembly;
*"I Am Malala: The Girl Who Stood Up For Education
and Was Shot by the Taliban")*

DEBATING THE ISSUES

"When you resort to attacking the messenger,
and not the message,
you have lost the debate."
--Addicon Whitcomb

ADOPTION MYTH #10
"Only those directly affected can effectively advocate"
"Hell hath no fury like a woman scorned
And Heaven hath no wrath
Like a Mother's love."
[Birth mothers have played an important, early role in advancing open records reform and other adoptee issues]
-Whisper

CHILDLESS, NOT COMPASSIONLESS

"WHY was Rachel Carson concerned about
the future of children?
She didn't have any children."
--Author Unknown
(Rachel Louise Carson, biologist, conservationist ,
advanced the global environmental movement,
authored *"Silent Spring."*)

THINKERS

"You can give a person knowledge
But you can't make them think.
Some people want to remain fools,
only because the truth requires change."
--Tony A. Gaskins Jr.

CAUSES

"We do not choose the causes
we believe in;
they choose us."
--Lori Carangelo, birth mother,
(founder, *"Americans For Open Records"-AmFOR*)

EXPRESSION

"Death is not the biggest fear we have;
our biggest fear is taking the risk to be alive
and express what we really are..."
--Don Miguel Ruiz, (*"Four Minute Books"*)

BE ACTIVIST

"Don't let complexity stop you.
Be activists. Take on the big inequities.
It will be one of the greatest experiences of your life."
--Bill Gates

WHAT MATTERS

"What matters in life
is not the mere fact that we have lived.
It is the difference we have made
to the lives of others
that will determine the significance
of the life we led."
--Nelson Mandela, 2002

THAT SMALL NOISY GROUP

"It does not require a majority to prevail
but rather an irate, tireless minority
keen to set brush fires in people's minds."
-Samuel Adams
(Note: *"That small noisy group"* is what Bill Pierce,
former Director, National Council For Adoption-
NCFA, called Adoption Activists)

COMMIT TO CHANGE

"Never doubt that a small group of thoughtful,
committed citizens can change the world;
indeed it is the only thing that ever has."
--Margaret Mead

MINORITY OF ONE

"…Even if you are a minority of one,
the truth is still the truth."
--Mahatma Gandhi

MOST POWERFUL, MOST IGNORED

"The voice of the adoptee
is the most powerful voice in adoption.
Yet it is the most overlooked
and ignored voice in adoption."
-(*"I Am Adopted"*)

FREEDOM

"Freedom is never given;
it is won."
--A. Philip Randolph

VIEWS

"We don't see things as they are,
We see them as we are."
-Anais Nin

UNPOPULAR VIEWS

"I'd rather run the risk of being disliked
for what I believe
than being liked
for what people think I believe."
-Ted Koppel, MSNBC-TV

LOST CAUSES

"Lost causes are the only ones
worth fighting for."
--Attorney Clarence Darrow

SUPPORT GROUPS

"We used to live in tribes.
And when there was a natural disaster
the tribe would sit around a fire and tell the story."
--Gloria Steinem, publisher *Ms. Magazine*,
founder, Feminist Party

FRIENDS AND ALLIES

"Friendship is born at that moment
when one person says to another
'What! You too? I thought I was the only one.'
--C.S. Lewis

POLITICAL CORRECTNESS

"Political correctness doesn't change us;
it shuts us up."
--Glenn Beck, American Journalist

CHANGE

"The ones who are 'crazy' enough
to think they can change the world
are the ones who do."
--Steve Jobs, adoptee, founder/CEO of
Apple Computer, and visionary (1955-2011)

JUST WRONG

"The way the federal government reimburses states
is to reward growth of the adoption programs,
instead of effective care of children."
--National Center for Policy

PAYING ATTENTION

"If the system doesn't make you angry,
you haven't been paying attention."
--Unknown

CALL IT WHAT IT IS

"Abducted, not adopted"
[re migrant children quietly being adopted
after their parents are deported.]"
--Saladin Ahmed, American author,
TheHill@theHill.com, 10-11-18

EMPOWERMENT

"Putting an end to secrecy in adoption
does not erase the grief or loss
embedded in the experience;
it does, however, empower participants
by providing them with the information and access
so that they can face and deal with the facts
instead of fantasies."
--Donaldson Adoption Institute
(*"Openness in Adoption,"* 2012)

WALK THE WALK

"If your path demands you to walk through Hell,
walk as if you own the place."
-Joe Soll, LCSW, adoptee
(*"Bar Stool"*)

TALK THE TALK

"When you feel like quitting
think about why you started."
-Joe Soll, LCSW, adoptee
(*"Power of Positivity"*)

1,000 TO 1

"There are a thousand hacking at the branches of evil
to one who is striking at the root."
--Henry David Thoreau

CIVIL DISOBEDIENCE

"Every immoral law must be disobeyed."
--Dr. Jack Kervorkian,
"right to die" activist

FOLLOWERS

"Be careful when you blindly follow the masses.
Sometimes the "m" is silent."
--Jessica On

NEVER GIVE UP

"Never give up
for that is just the place and time
that the tide may turn."
--Harriet Beecher Stowe

3 KINDS OF LIES

"There are 3 kinds of lies:
lies, damned lies, and statistics."
--Benjamin Disraeli,
British Prime Minister, 1874-1880

HELL

"Hell is truth seen too late."
--Thomas Hobbs

BLOOD TIES

"Adoption attempts to nullify blood ties."
--Mary Louise Foess, adoptee,
(Founder, "*Bonding By Blood Unlimited*")

UNHEALTHY

"Adoption is unhealthy for children
and other living things."
--Jess DelBalzo,
(founder *"Adoption: Legalized Lies"*)

ADOPTION REDIRECTION

"Love children. Adopt pets."
--Jess DelBalzo
(founder, *"Adoption: Legalized Lies"*)

MIND AND HEART

"One sure measure
of the mind and heart of any society
is how it treats its children."
–Loring Brace,
initiator of the Orphan Trains

LOUDEST VOICES

"Adoption will never be the same
as long as 'birth' mothers of the past
have their loud say about how it is practiced.
The intense trauma of their experience
has been boiling under the surface
of their lives for many years
and they will never again be silenced."
--Anonymous

APPONO ASTOS

"'Appono Astos,'
--Celtic Crop Circle message –
(Translation :
We are opposed to cunning and deceit.")

ADOPTION COLONIALISM

"Adoption is a form of colonialism."
--Jean Paton, MA/MSW (1908-2002)
("*The Adopted Break Silence*")

CLOSED ADOPTION,
CLOSED MINDS

"Closed adoption is institutionalized denial."
--Nancy Murray, LCSW,
Placement Supervisor,
("*The Whole Family*")

OPEN ADOPTION

"Open adoption, to me,
means love, respect and family."
--Brooke Glassburn

CHILD STEALERS

"Adoption is geopolitical mass child stealing."
--Eugene Austin (1922-2015)
aka "Mean Gene," family rights activist

IMMIGRATION:
ADOPTION ABDUCTION

"Illegal foreign adoption:
shortcut to immigration."
--Shoneen Gervich, adoptive mother

PROGRESS

"The reasonable man adapts himself to the world;
the unreasonable man persists in
trying to adapt the world to himself.
Therefore, all progress depends
on the unreasonable man."
--George Bernard Shaw

HOW FAR?

"The human soul is difficult to interfere with--
You hesitate how far you should go."
--Loring Brace, initiator of the Orphan Trains

EXIST FOR OTHERS

"Only a life lived for others
is a life worthwhile....
Without deep reflection, one knows
from daily life,
that one exists for other people."
--Albert Einstein

COMMON GOOD

"Forced groups are invariably less efficient
than free groups working for the common good."
--L. Ron Hubbard (*"Dianetics"*)

TRY

"Every Accomplishment
starts with the decision to try."
--President John F. Kennedy

WHY NOT?

"There are those who look at things
and ask 'Why?'...
I dream of things that never were
And ask 'Why not?'"
--Robert F. Kennedy

NEVER FAIL TO PROTEST

"There may be times when men are powerless
to prevent injustice.
But there must never be a time
when we fail to protest."
--Elie Wiesel

VISIONARY

"The way a visionary works--he moves on,
but he leaves a lot of ideas behind.
It's like science fiction.
Someone writes about a world but they
don't actually create it.
They leave a map for others to follow...
I like options....
You're as young as the last time you
changed your mind."
--Timothy Leary
("*Timothy Leary Celebrates Dying,*"
Los Angeles Times, 2-28-95)

UNTIL PROVEN

"All things are possible
until they are proven impossible--
and even the impossible may only be so as of now."
--Pearl S. Buck, adopter, 1930's newspaper columnist
who advocated "*forever separating
the unwed mother from her child.*"

IMPOSSIBLE DOESN'T EXIST

"The word 'impossible' is not in my dictionary."
--Napolean Bonaparte

BECAUSE YOU MUST

"You must do the things you think you cannot do."
--First Lady Eleanor Roosevelt

SO JUST DO IT

"Do it! What are you waiting on? Do it!
Stand up for what you believe in.
The world needs your voice.
Whoever you are, you have something to say.
Say it."
--Kerry Washington

TIMING

"Timing is everything."
--Leah Rae, Bob Hope's first leading lady

MORAL OR RIGHT?

"Never let your sense of morals
get in the way of
doing what is right."
--Isaac Asimov

WORTH IT

"Everything I did in my life
that was worthwhile
I caught hell for."
--Chief Justice Earl Warren

VICES

"The problem with people
who have no vices
is that generally you can be pretty sure
they're going to have
some pretty annoying virtues."
--Elizabeth Taylor

FIGHT, REPEAT

"You may have to fight a battle
more than once to win it."
--Margaret Thatcher,
Prime Minister of Great Britain

CRITICAL THINKING

"If you think you can, you can,
and if you think you can't,
you're right."
--Mary Ash, Mary Kay Cosmetics

ANGER

"I'm red in the face
My hands are clenched in tight fists
Fists formed by the past
A past filled with hate
Expected to forget
The unjustifying crimes
I clench my fists
Taken, [like property, not people]
Families, sold apart
Still divided I clench my fists
I'm more bruised, I'm beaten
My fists swell and explode
The past pours out of me
My fists...my expression
I empty my rage
The blood drains from my face
I rise up through the anger."
--Adapted from poem about Slavery, by
Brian Hoyer, Julia Schafer and Vicky Hoehn

REALITY CHECK

"Remember, no matter where you go,
there you are."
--Urban Cubbage

RECHANNELING

"I forgave my father who raped me.
But I denied the man who held my redemption.
If we walk only on sunny days,
we never reach our destination
but remain between Heaven and Earth."
--Oliver Stone (*"Heaven and Earth"*)

RIGHT TO KNOW

"Isn't people wanting to know their origins
more important than people not wanting to know
their own offspring?
Don't the original parents have a moral obligation
to acknowledge their own kids?
--Penny Partridge, adoptee, adopter, and activist for
open adoption records
I know of no safe depository
of the ultimate powers of society
but the people themselves.
And if we think them not enlightened enough
to exercise their control with a wholesome discretion,
the remedy is not to take it from them,
but to inform their discretion."
--Thomas Jefferson,
(who fathered children
by his slave, Sally Hemmings)

EXISTENCE

"There's something in us
that wants the world to know we existed."
-(Unknown)

AVOIDANCE

"It's when you run away
you're most likely to stumble."
--Ernest Hemingway

CHILD'S BEST INTERESTS

"A child's 'best interests'
are not served by special interests.
--Arthur Sorosky, MD, UCLA, 1989

BETTER TO KNOW

"I believe it is better to tell the truth than a lie.
I believe it is better to be free than a slave.
And I believe it is better to know
than to be ignorant."
--H.L. Mencken, newspaper mogul

KNOWING

"Know Thyself."
--Inscription of the Delphi Oracle

NO WAITING

"How wonderful it is
that no one needs to wait a single moment
before starting to improve the world."
--Anne Frank
("Anne Frank's Tales From The Secret Annex")

SCARS

"Our scars have the power
to revisit our pasts."
--Anonymous

THE PAST

"The past isn't dead...
it isn't even past."
--William Faulkner

ERASED

"Alienating a child
from his biological family
is exactly the same
as erasing part of the child."
--ariaappleford.com

DRAWING THE LINE

"An empty blackboard stands alone;
they erased who I was and gave me a new home.
Liquid paper where my life used to be;
how could they take that away from me?
Did they really believe I'd never question
what they gave me as a definition
of the person I was supposed to become,
and never look back on where I came from?
Where does one really draw the line
on how much past you can leave behind?
They expect of us what they themselves could not do.
Despite what they say, I am searching--
Wouldn't you?"
--Karen Joiner, adoptee (*"Erased"*)

WALLS

"Before I built a wall I'd ask to know
What I was walling in or walling out,
And to whom I was like to give offense.
Something there is that doesn't love a wall,
That wants to tear it down."
--Robert Frost (*"The Mending Wall"*)

SECRECY

"All sins are committed in secrecy.
The moment we realize that
God witnessed our thoughts
We shall be free."
--Mahatma Gandhi

PUBLIC OPINION

"There is not a crime,
there is not a vice,
which does not live in secrecy.
Get these things out in the open,
describe them,
attack them,
ridicule them in the press
and sooner or later
public opinion will
sweep them away."
--John Pulitzer

IGNORANCE IS BLISS

"After placement with adoptive parents,
we must assume 'no news is good news.'"
--Eunice Baker, Adoptions Caseworker,
The Children's Center, Hamden, Connecticut,
(responding to Lori Carangelo's letter asking if her
child was *actually* adopted, alive and well.)

DISTRUST GOVERNMENT

"Secrecy in government
has become synonymous,
in the public mind,
with deception in government."
--Lawton Mainor Charles, Jr., U.S. Senator, 11-4-75

CONSPIRACY THEORY

"Secrecy, being an instrument of conspiracy,
ought never to be the system of a regular government."
--Jeremy Bentham, English philosopher

AWARENESS

"As awareness increases,
the need for personal secrecy
almost proportionately decreases."
--Charlotte Painter
("*Revelations: Diaries of Women*")

IMPORTANCE OF KNOWING

"If you combine lying and secrecy,
and if you also bring in violence,
then I think a republic can die.
I don't think it's possible
for citizens to have much of an effect
if they literally don't know what's going on.
--Sissela Bok ("*A World of Ideas*," 1989)

CRIME OF ILLEGITIMACY

"Obviously the 'crime of illegitimacy'
is not pardonable in the state of Missouri."
--James Grant George, adoptee
(When a Judge denied disclosure
from his adoption file to seek a biological relative
as potential bone marrow donor to save his life)

CRIME OF LOVE

"Love if not a felony. So open records."
--Emily Bernhardt, adoptee

HUMAN

"Cruelty has a human interest,
And Jealousy a human face;
Terror, the human form divine,
And Secrecy, the human dress."
--William Blake
(*"Songs of Experience: A Divine Image"*)

IT'S NOT COMPLICATED

"No more secrets,
no more lies!"
--Ginni D. Snodgrass, adoptee
and Activist for open records

TRUTH

"Indeed, the truth shall set you free."
--("*Jeremiah 10:19*" and "*John 8:3,*" *The Bible*)

COVER UP

"Everybody knows that corruption thrives
in secret places....
and we believe it a fair presumption
that secrecy means impropriety."
--President Thomas Woodrow Wilson

GOVERNMENT

"Secrecy and a free democratic government don't mix.
--Merle Miller ("*Plain Speaking*")

ABUSE

"Sealed records are a form of child abuse."
--Sharon Kaplan, BSW, MS, adoptive mother,
(founder, "*Parenting Resources*")

RIGHTS

"A right is not a right, in America,
unless it extends to all Americans."
--Archibald Cox, Special Prosecutor,
"*Watergate*" - Impeachment of Richard Nixon

ADOPTEE RIGHTS

"Adoptee rights are human rights."
--Lori Carangelo, founder,
"Americans For Open Records" - AmFOR

STUMBLE HAND IN HAND

"Remember, we all stumble,
every one of us.
That's why it's a comfort
to go hand in hand."
--Emily Kimbrough

FREEDOM

"At every stage in social development,
freedom has to be re-conquered."
--Sir Lewis Namier

ADOPTION TERRORISM

"Adoption is a form of domestic terrorism."
--Reverend Ruth Peterson

NO FEAR

"Do what you fear
and the fear goes away."
--Ralph Waldo Emerson

BUYING A STATE OF MIND

"Psychiatry is full of technical terms,
and if a criminal is rich enough,
he generally finds experts to qualify his state of mind
with a sufficient number of technical terms
to over-awe those used to scrutinizing authorities
and their discretionary powers."
--Morris R. Cohen

IMPOSSIBLE

"Most of the things worth doing in this world
had been declared impossible before they were done."
-Louis D. Brandeis, U.S. Supreme Court Justice

OBSTACLES

"We who lived in the concentration camps
can remember the men who walked through the huts
comforting others,
giving away their last piece of bread.
They may have been few in number,
but they offer sufficient proof
that everything can be taken from a man but one thing:
The last of his freedoms –
to choose one's attitude
in any given set of circumstances,
to choose one's own way."
-Victor E. Frankl ("*Man's Search for Meaning*")

A FREE PRESS

"First among priorities of a free press
was exposing the secrets of government."
--U.S. Supreme Court Justice Hugo Black,
as quoted by Bob Woodward
and Scott Armstrong ("*The Brethren*")

RIGHT TO RECEIVE INFORMATION

"There is a right to receive information,
regardless of its social worth,
regardless of its obscenity."
--U.S. Supreme Court Justice Thomas Brennan,
as quoted by Bob Woodward
and Scott Armstrong ("*The Brethren*")

ADOPTION GAME

"Our governments play games with adults."
--Judith Brans, adoptee,
founder, "*Parent Finders,*" Ontario, Canada

PURPOSE

"The mystery of human existence
lies not in just staying alive,
but in finding something to live for."
--Fyodor Dostoyevsky

8.
ADOPTION
AUTHORS

THE MIGHTY PEN

"You own everything that happened to you.
Publish your own story.
If people wanted you to write warmly about them,
They should have behaved better."
-Unknown

WHY WRITE?

"Since I'm an educator, I'm biased: More education will usually seem to me to be the answer not only for outsiders thinking about or interacting with adoptive families and for people contemplating adoption. The more experience we have – both personal experience and the vicarious experience we can get through researching accounts of adoptions in the present and the past – the easier we'll find it to move away from stereotypes, false assumptions and unrealistic expectations."
--Claudia Nelson, adoptee, author,
("Little Strangers – Portrayal of Adoption and Foster Care in America, 1850-1929")

RE-EXPERIENCING THE SCRIPT

"We write to taste life twice,
in the moment and in retrospect."
--Anais Nin

THE UNTOLD STORY

"There is no greater agony
than bearing an untold story inside you."
– Maya Angelou

A PERSON EXPLAINED

"Each of us is a book waiting to be written;
and that book, if written,
results in a person explained."
–Thomas M. Cirignann
(*"The Constant Outsider"*)

YOU ARE UNIQUE

"I'm a theatre professional who has educated myself on the complexities of adoption after relinquishing my only child in 2010. Since my son was born, I've spent my time cultivating a relationship with my son and his adoptive parents - a gay couple who also lived in NYC. And I spend some of my spare time trying to educate others about what open adoption can be and what my experience as a birth parent has been."
--Deanna Binkofky, birth mother,
(contributing author, *"It's Not About You:
Understanding Adoptee Search, Reunion & Open
Adoption"*)

MEMOIR

"I've looked at life
from both sides now
from win and lose
and still somehow
it's life's illusions I recall;
I really don't know life at all."
-Joni Mitchell

MEMORIALIZING

"Grief starts to become indulgent,
and it doesn't serve anyone,
and it's painful.
But if you transform it into remembrance,
then you're magnifying the person you've lost
and also giving something of that person
to other people,
so they can experience something of that person."
–Patti Smith

INTROSPECTION

""Death is not the biggest fear we have;
the biggest fear is taking the risk to be alive
and expressing what we really are."
--Don Miguel Ruiz

CATHARSIS

"Tears are words
that need to be written."
--Paula Coelho

CONTROVERSY

"Let us welcome
controversial books
and controversial authors."
--John F. Kennedy

THE TITLE

"A good title
is the title of a successful book."
-Raymond Chandler

FIRST DRAFT

"The first draft
is just you
telling yourself the story."
--Terry Pratchett

CHAPTER ONE

"You can't start
the next chapter
of your life
if you keep re-reading
the last one."
–Loveasagame.com

NEXT CHAPTER

"I may not have gone where I intended to go
but I think I've ended up where I needed to be."
–Douglas Adams,
("*The Long Dark Tea-Time of the Soul*" and
"*The Ultimate Hitchhiker's Guide to the Galaxy*")

THE PLOT

"Plot is people.
Human emotions and desires
founded in the realities of life,
working at cross purposes,
getting better and fiercer,
as they strike against each other
and finally there's an explosion –
that's the Plot."
--Leigh Brackett

THE PLOT THICKENS

"The two most important days of your life
are the day you were born
and the day you find out why."
–Mark Twain

WRITER'S BLOCK

"You can always edit a bad page.
You can't edit a blank page."
--Jodi Picoult

ME, MYSELF AND I

"I almost always urge people
to write in the first person…
Writing is an act of ego
And you might as well admit it."
--William Zinsset

THE AUTOBIOGRAPHY

"Every secret of a writer's soul,
every experience of his life,
every quality of his mind,
is written large in his work."
--Virginio Woolf

THE END

"There is no real ending.
It's just the place where you stop the story."
--Frank Herbert

BOOK REVIEWS

"Authors always take rejection badly -
They equate it with infanticide."
–P.D. James

A WRITER'S ADDICTION

"Some drink,
some do drugs.
I write."
–Pamela Morris,
("That's What Shadows Are Made Of")

BIBLIOGRAPHY

Anderson, Robert, "*Second Choice: Growing Up Adopted,*"
Badger Hill, 1993

Baran, Annette; and Pannor, Reuben, "*Lethal Secrets,*"
Warner Books, 1989; "*The Adoption Triangle: Effects of
Sealed Records on Adoptees, Birthparents and Adoptive
Parents,*" Baran, Pannor, Sorosky, 1984

Belkin, Lisa, "*Michael and His 3 Parents: The First Open
Adoption Babies Come of Age,*" Yahoo News, 12-15-18

Benet, Mary K, "*The Politics of Adoption,*" The Free Press,
1976

Bouchard, Thomas J., et al, "*Sources of Human Psychological
Differences: The Minnesota Study of Twins Reared
Apart,*" Science Magazine (1990; and 1979-1990 study
of over 100 twin pairs; 500 more twin pairs were
added in Y-2000)

Bradshaw, John, "*Family Secrets: What You Don't Know Can
Hurt You,*" Bantam, 1955

Brodzinsky, David M., Schecter, Henig, "*Being Adopted - The
Lifelong Search For Self,*" Doubleday, 1992

Carlis, Tracy L., PhD, "*The Resulting Effect of In Utero
Attachment on the Personality Development of an
Adopted Individual.*"Carp, E. Wayne, "*Jean Paton and
the Struggle for Adoption Reform,* " University of
Michigan Press, 2014.

Coppinger, Maureen, "*Annie's Girl –How An Abandoned
Orphan Finally Discovered the Truth About Her
Mother*"

Crawford, Christina, "*Mommie Dearest,*" Berkley Publishing,
1984

D'Arcy, Claudia Corrigan, "*National Council for Adoption:
Mothers, Money, Marketing and Madness.*"

Denfield, Rene, "*The Other Missing Children Scandal:
Thousands of Lost American Foster Kids,*" The
Washington Post, 6-18-18

Deykin, E, "*Post-Adoptive Experience of Surrendering Parents,*"
American Journal of Orthopsychiatry, 1986

Edwards, Hefen, and Jenny Lee Smith, *"My Secret Sister
        - Separated at Birth, One Sister Abused, One Loved*

Eldridge, Sherrie, *"Twenty Things Adopted Kids Wish Their
        Adoptive Parents Knew,"* Dell Books, 1999

Ezell, Lee, *"The Missing Piece,"* Bantam Books, 1986

Faririsi, Theresa Rodrigues, *"When Adoption Fails,"*
        Housekeepers Publishing, 2000

Fessler, Ann, *"The Girls Who Went Away,"* Penguin, 2000

Goldstein, J; Freud, A; Solnit, A.J., *"Beyond the Best Interests of
        the Child,"* Free Press, 1973

Kluger Jeffrey, *"The Sibling Effect – What the Bonds Among
        Brothers and Sisters Reveal About Us"*

Kirk, David H., *"Shared Fate: A Theory and Method of Adoptive
        Relationships,"* Ben-Simon, 1985

Kirschner, David, PhD, *"Adoption: Uncharted Waters,"* 2006

Kittson, Rutheen (aka Jean Paton), *"Orphan Voyage,"*
        1951

Lehman, Robert, *"Young Unwed Fathers: Changing Roles,"*
        Temple University Press, 1993

Lifton, Betty Jean, *"Journey of the Adopted Self,"* Basic Books,
        1994; *"Lost and Found: The Adoption Experience; Twice
        Born: Memoirs of An Adopted Daughter,"* Penguin,
        1977

MacKenzie, Tom H., *"The Last Foundling- The True Story of a
        Kidnapping, a Family Secret and My Search for the Real
        Me"*

Neubauer, Peter B., *"Twins/Triplets Study,"* unpublished,
        Yale University Archives, sealed until October 25,
        2065; Basis for CNN Film for TV *"Three Identical
        Strangers,"* Jan-Feb 2019

Nixon, Ron, *"U.S. Loses Track of Another 1500 Migrant
        Children, Investigators Find,"* New York Times,
        9-18-18.

Paton, Jean, *"The Adopted Break Silence: Forty Men and Women
        Describe Their Search for Their Natural Parents,"* Life
        Study Center, 1954

Pertman, Adam, *"Adoption Nation: How the Adoption
        Revolution is Transforming America,"* Basic Books 2000

Plomin, *"Blueprint: How DNA Makes Us Who We Are,"*

Reagan, Michael; with Hyams, Joe, *"On the Outside Looking In*, Zebra, 1998

Randolph, Brooke, *"It's Not About You – Understanding Adoptee Search, Reunion and Open Adoption,"* Entourage Publishing, 2017

Riben, Marsha, *"Shedding Light on the Dark Side of Adoption,"* Harlo Press, 1988

Robinson, Evelyn Burns, *"Adoption and Loss: The Hidden Grief,"* Clova Publications, 2005

Solinger, Rickie, *"Wake Up Little Susie: Single Pregnancy & Race Before Roe v. Wade,"* Routledge , 1992; *"Beggars And Choosers: How Politics of Choice Shape Adoption, Abortion and Welfare in the United States,"* Hill and Wang, 2002

Soll, Joe, LCSW, DAPA, *"Adoption Healing – A Path To Recovery,"* 2000-2013 series

Stewart, Sara, *"Separated-at-Birth Triplets Met Tragic End After Shocking Experiment,'* New York Post, 6-23-18

Stiffler, Lavonne Harper, *"Synchronicity & Reunion,"*

Verrier, Nancy, *"Primal Wound, Understanding the Adopted Child,"* Story 1983, Triumph Press, 1979

Wilson-Buterbaugh, *"The Baby Scoop Era: Unwed Mothers, Infant Adoption, Forced Surrender"* Amazon Books, 2017

INDEX

ABOUT THE AUTHOR

In 1969 Lori Carangelo lost her 6-week old son to unintended sealed adoption. After almost 2 decades of unsuccessfully searching for him, she reunited with him in 1987 when he was 18. Now 75, she and her son, now 50, maintained their relationship for 30 years.

Retired in the 1980s from administrative positions in Santa Barbara and Palm Desert, California, Lori devoted the next 20 years to helping adoptees and birth families to reconnect, *without charge*, via "Americans For Open Records" (AmFOR), her national network of volunteer searchers, producing some of the first reunions highlighting adoption issues on TV and radio talk shows, and in newspaper feature stories. AmFOR also lobbied for open records and other adoption reforms.

With the data gleaned from the reunions, and her research, she served as Data Source to the United Nations Rights of the Child Project. Her research also supported her adoption-linked "true crime" books to answer "why" they did it.

"Carangelo v. Connecticut" documents her case, argued for 4 years in U.S. District Court of Connecticut; in 1993, the U. S. Supreme Court filed the case, but declined to address constitutionality of *"government protected child stealing under color of state sealed records law."* Attorneys later commented that the High Court was simply *"not ready"* for that issue.

163

More Books by Lori Carangelo:

THE ULTIMATE SEARCH BOOK –
U.S. & Worldwide Editions
Adoption, Genealogy and Other Search Secrets
THE ADOPTION and DONOR CONCEPTION FACTBOOK
The Only Comprehensive Source of U.S. & Global Data
On the Invisible Families of Adoption, Foster Care & Donor Conception
CHOSEN CHILDREN
People, Politics and America's Failed Foster Care
and Adoption Industries
ADOPTION UNCENSORED
4 Decades of Politics, People and Commentary
CARANGELO v. CONNECTICUT
A Case of Lifelong Opposition to Government Protected Child Stealing
BLOOD RELATIVES
A True Story of Family Secrets and Murders
8 BALL CAFÉ
Stories of Adoption, Addiction and Redemption
KONDRO
The Untold Story of the Longview Serial Killer
KILLERS ONLINE
100 True Stories
SERIAL KILLERS ON THE INTERSTATE
100 Highway Killers, By State
RAGE!
How An Adoption Ignited Fire
ADOPTED KILLERS
430 Adoptees Who Killed – How and Why They Did It
FRAMED!
The Carefully Crafted Central Coast Rapist
ESPOSITO
The First Mafioso
FROM ITALIAN AMERICA with LOVE (Cookbook)
FROM ITALY and ALL NATIONS with LOVE (Cookbook)

www.ingramcontent.com/pod-product-compliance
Lightning Source LLC
Chambersburg PA
CBHW061724020426
42331CB00006B/1075